This Walker book belongs to:

....

....

For Tage, Savva, Kaia, Gregor-David — K. H.

For Sam, James and Beatrice — P. H.

First published 2006 by Walker Books Ltd

87 Vauxhall Walk, London SE11 5HJ

This edition published 2008

1 2 3 4 5 6 7 8 9 10

Text © 2006 Kathy Henderson

Illustrations © 2006 Paul Howard

This book has been typeset in FC Contemporay Brush

Printed in China

British Library Cataloguing in Publication Data: a catalogue record
for this book is available from the British Library

ISBN 978-1-4063-0459-6

www.walkerbooks.co.uk

LOOK at YOU!

WOW, WHAT A BODY CAN DO!

Kathy Henderson

illustrated by **Paul Howard**

WALKER BOOKS
AND SUBSIDIARIES
LONDON · BOSTON · SYDNEY · AUCKLAND

Fingers and toes
wiggle.

Eyes, nose and mouth giggle.

Arms wave, legs kick ...

bottoms squirm ...
    and tummies tickle.

Clothes on.

Where's the baby gone?

There
he is!

Clothes off!

Where are the baby's toes?

There they are!

Lie

roll

sit

wobble.

Rock

crawl

pull

wobble.

Stand

wobble

sway

wobble.

Bump!

Step

walk

toddle!

What can you see?

Something to eat.

What can you hear?

A song in the air.

What can you smell?

мmmmm! Food.

How does it taste?

Good,

good,

good.

And how does it feel?
Warm and squelchy, scratchy, rough, sticky, squishy...

Time for a bath!

Float

soap

splash

wash

slide

glide

cuddle

brush.

Clip, snip, some things grow quick.

Hey ho, others grow slow!

Funny thing, hair...
You can brush it this way,
you can brush it that,
wash it, dry it, tie it up
and squash it flat.

I feel ...

good,

bad,

happy,

sad,

bold,

shy
(I don't
know why).

I feel lonely.

I feel fine.

A-a-a-chooo!

Wow, what a body can do!

Yawn! Hic! Plenty of tricks.

Whoops!
Pooh!

Wow, what a body can do!

Sigh, flop, snuggle down,
curl up in a heap.

The story's done, this body's tired
and now it's going to sleep.

Other books by Kathy Henderson

ISBN 978-1-4063-0965-2

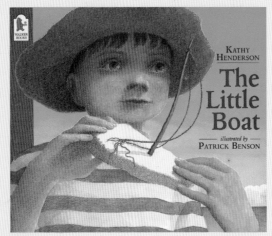

ISBN 978-0-7445-5253-9

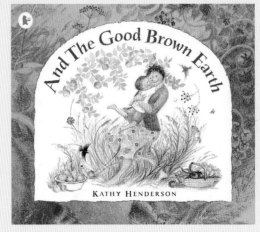

ISBN 978-1-84428-558-7

Also by Paul Howard

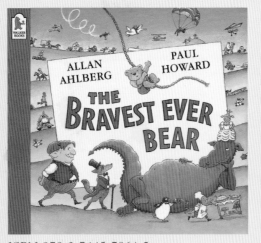

ISBN 978-0-7445-7864-5

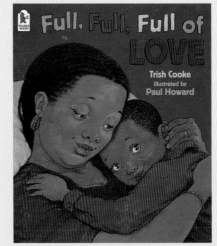

ISBN 978-1-84428-782-6

AVAILABLE FROM ALL GOOD BOOKSTORES

www.walkerbooks.co.uk

For Mum & Dad – R.I.
For my Nana – L.H.

EGMONT

First published in Great Britain 2021 by Egmont Books

An imprint of HarperCollins*Publishers*
1 London Bridge Street
London SE1 9GF

www.egmontbooks.co.uk

Text copyright © Rachel Ip 2021
Illustrations copyright © Laura Hughes 2021

The moral rights of the author and illustrator have been asserted.

ISBN 978 1 4052 9476 8
70284/001
Printed in China.

A CIP catalogue record for this book is available from the British Library.

Amelia's Granny was forgetful.

Sometimes she forgot little things. Like where she'd put the marmalade or which drawer she kept her socks in.

Sometimes she forgot important things like special memories and moments.

Amelia was forgetful too, because she
was very busy daydreaming and exploring.

One day, Amelia and Granny were both so busy exploring
that they completely forgot to go home for dinner.

They wandered deep into the forest.

And that's when they found The Forgettery.

"What *is* this place?" said Amelia.
"What's a Forgettery?"

"Let's find out!" said Granny.

The Forgettery

Now, some people don't believe in The Forgettery.
And some people have simply forgotten about it.
But for those who believe, it's a place where you
can find *anything* you have ever forgotten.

"Welcome to The Forgettery,"
said a tall man on roller skates.
"I'm one of the Memory Keepers.
We look after forgotten memories."

"We've forgotten the way home,"
said Amelia.

"Don't worry – we have everything
you have *ever* forgotten.
Maps, moments, memories . . .
Climb aboard!"

"Let's find your memories,
Granny!" said Amelia,
as they soared into the air.

They rose
higher and higher
until they arrived at a door
with Granny's name on it.

Granny's Forgettery was huge because she was very forgetful.

She smiled as her memories washed around her.

Moments of delight,
lost and forgotten, fluttering in the room
like butterflies. Paper thin and delicate.

The smell of fresh bread.

The sound of autumn leaves, crackling underfoot.

The sheer giddiness of a cartwheel.

Her most secret hiding place and her favourite blue dress.

"It's *so* hard to choose," said Granny,
"but these are my most treasured
memories."

She carefully picked out her favourite moments.

"What a magical place," said Granny, her cheeks flushed with excitement. "So many happy memories came flooding back to me."

Outside in the corridor, they saw a signpost to Amelia's Forgettery. They climbed up and up, and squeezed inside.

It was cosy and warm and
much smaller than Granny's.

There was an entire box of forgotten
'please and thank yous'.

you you
you th you
Thank you
Thank you

All the 'which way rounds' of
her gloves and shoes and socks.
Amelia giggled . . .

right   Left

And in the corner,
a box of ouches, bumps and grazes,
she was pleased she'd forgotten.

Suddenly, there was a delivery.

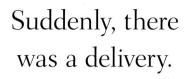

They had *completely* forgotten the time! They had to get back home before dinner.

When they reached the ground
floor, the Memory Keeper
was waiting for them.

"Thank you," said Amelia,
"For an unforgettable day!"

"Don't forget
The Way Home," he said,
handing Granny a map.
"And this is for *you*,
Amelia."

When they got home, Amelia started making a book with all the memories Granny had collected at The Forgettery.

She added names and photos to help Granny remember.

The Forgettery
Memory Making Advice

Share laughter, share a book, share a picnic.

Play games, play together, play outside.

Take a photo, write a story, draw a picture.

Make friends, make a sandcastle, make a den.

And when you least expect it, you will make

a memory!

Amelia

Every time they did something fun together,
Amelia took a photo, and added it to the memory book.

They loved looking at the book together.

"Look, here's the day we went to The Forgettery!"
said Amelia.

Granny smiled.
"I have one more thing for *you*
to remember . . .

Thinking
of you

TREES

. . . I'll always love you."

"And I'll always love you," said Amelia.
"That's something I'll *never* forget."

The
Forgettery
Memory-Making Advice

Share laughter, share a book, share a picnic.
Play games, play together, play outside.
Take a photo, write a story, draw a picture.
Make friends, make a sandcastle, make a den.
And when you least expect it, you will make

a memory!